FIND YOUR POWER

MANIFEST

An Hachette UK Company
www.hachette.co.uk

First published in Great Britain in 2023 by Godsfield,
an imprint of Octopus Publishing Group Ltd
Carmelite House, 50 Victoria Embankment, London EC4Y 0DZ
www.octopusbooks.co.uk

ISBN 978-1-8418-1539-8

A CIP catalogue record for this book is available from the British Library

Printed and bound in China

10 9 8 7 6 5 4 3 2 1

Publisher: Lucy Pessell
Designer: Isobel Platt
Senior Editor: Hannah Coughlin
Assistant Editor: Samina Rahman
Production Controller: Allison Gonsalves

FIND YOUR POWER

MANIFEST

ANOUSHKA F. CHURCHILL

GODSFIELD

CONTENTS

INTRODUCTION   8

PRACTISING HAPPINESS   32

EMBRACING THE PRESENT   46

MEETING THE FUTURE   62

NOURISHING THE PAST   76

CREATING THE PLAN   90

LIVING THE DREAM   108

FIND
YOUR
POWER

When daily life becomes busy and your time and energy is pulled in many different directions, it can be difficult to find time to nourish yourself. Prioritizing your own wellbeing can be a struggle and you risk feeling overwhelmed, unsure of where to turn and what you need in order to feel lighter and find your inner strength.

Taking some time to focus on yourself, answering questions you may be avoiding or facing problems that are simmering away under the surface is the best gift you can give yourself. But it can be difficult to know where to start.

Sometimes all you need to learn life's big lessons is a little guidance. In this series of books you will learn about personal healing, self empowerment and how to nourish your spirit. Explore practices which will help you to get clear on what you really want, and that will encourage you to acknowledge – and deal with – any limiting beliefs or negative thoughts that might be holding you back to living life to your fullest power.

These pocket-sized books provide invaluable advice on how to create the best conditions for a healthier, happier, and more fulfilled life Bursting with essential background, revealing insights and useful activities and exercises to enable yourself to understand and expand your personal practices every day, it's time to delve into your spiritual journey and truly Find Your Power.

Other titles in the series:
- *Find Your Power: Tarot*
- *Find Your Power: Runes*
- *Find Your Power: Numerology*

INTRODUCTION

You can have what you want.

Read that sentence again. Say it to yourself, if you can; say it aloud, say it slowly, say it with purpose. Say it deliberately, and – if you can – mean it.

I can have what I want.

How does that make you feel?

More to the point, did you bring yourself even to try it?

Could you – when it came to it – say it out loud?

If you did, could you say it *and* mean it?

Did it make you feel foolish or silly or selfish?

Oh, don't beat yourself up about it. If we could all say it, and mean it, and know that we meant it, there wouldn't be any reason for this book to exist.

This book rests on this simple little statement: six words that are easy to type, hard to say and almost impossible to mean. You can find your power in manifesting, and it is a promise that you can have what you want. More than that: a promise that you can have what you *need*.

BEST
SELF BOX

Manifestation is an investment in the self. A Best Self Box is a tangible reminder, right from the start, of that investment. For the exercises in this book, you'll need several things – and I recommend you bring them together into a Best Self Box. This is the box in which your new life begins, and it's going to contain all the supplies you need. You'll gather some things over the chapters within, but it's best to start somewhere – and this way, you'll have what you need to hand.

The Best Self Box can be any kind of container that's just for you, but I'd encourage you to take it seriously. Choose something beautiful. Choose something that represents the place where you'd like your life to end up: a jewellery box, a perfectly shaded glass food container (with matching lid), a shoebox from a fancy shoe store or something you make yourself. You could wrap it in brown paper (my personal choice: classy neutral eco-future for me, please!) or beautiful artisan wrapping paper; you could papier-mâché it with pages from magazines and old books you love. You could do anything.

This may sound silly – but a lot of manifestation is about encouraging the creative, the beautiful and the playful in your life. Much of this book will encourage you to tap into this indulgent, silly, artsy self: we want to be at our most confident, most playful and most thoughtful. And we want to express that. So much of manifesting is about bringing our outer reality in line with our inner mind; and art is a wonderful way to express that.

This book will live in the box, at least until you've finished working with it – and so will your

Manifestation Journal. This is the most important thing in the box: I'd like you to find a journal that makes you feel like your best self. A journal that your future self might have. The kind of journal that maybe you've always been too afraid to write in, in case you spoil it.

To go alongside the journal, you'll need some craft supplies. These are just for you – not to share with anyone else, even if you have kids who would love to have a go with your sharp scissors or beautiful colouring pencils! These craft supplies are your investment in your own creativity and spark, and you deserve them, too. Maybe you want every colour of washi tape. Maybe you want brand-name adhesives that will stick things down and keep them stuck. Stickers, even. Good pens that are nice to write with. These don't have to be expensive – but you are allowed to treat yourself sometimes. Consider this permission if you need it.

I'd like you also to choose a couple of essential oils, or perhaps just a perfume or sprig of lavender for the box. Scent is such a good way to bring us in touch with our physical bodies, and some – like lavender – have been scientifically proven to aid relaxation and clarity. If the box smells gorgeous, we're more likely to keep it near us.

Please remember: you deserve beautiful things. This book is all about beautiful things – and that includes you.

This book is all about beautiful things – and that includes you.

THERE IS
ENOUGH FOR
EVERYONE

We live in a world of abundance. There is more than enough to go round; there is enough for everyone. This is not a metaphor: this is literally, practically true. A United Nation report tells us that we could feed everyone who exists – and well – with what the planet can give us. The Earth provides; the universe provides. There is enough food, there is enough money and there is enough time. There is enough love.

And yet, somehow, it never plays out that way.

And it never *feels* that way.

Our world is one of plenty – masquerading as one of scarcity. Even the luckiest among us – and I count you and I, reading and writing this book respectively, among their number – are scrabbling for satisfaction. We try our best, and yet it slips away from us: we want the things we can't have, and don't have the things we need. Who do you know who feels they get *enough*? When was the last time you felt *enough*?

We try to mask this feeling. Maybe we swing wildly from total self-indulgence to strict self-denial; our culture certainly fetishizes both. We live in a boom-and-bust economy, shackled by diet culture, dragged down by patriarchy and racism, shaped by the whiplash-inducing cycle of decadence and starvation. For women, in particular, it sometimes feels that there is no way to win. Eat more, eat less; do more, do less; be more, be less. You are too much. You are not enough. Whatever we do, whoever we are, we have something to apologize for. We have something we ought to hide. We have something we ought to be ashamed of.

We are taught every day, consciously and subconsciously, that we don't deserve the things we want.

Are you tired of living like this?

We are told to repress and suppress our desires, our needs and our ambition. We are asked to minimize ourselves, physically and mentally, so that we don't take up too much space. We are taught every day, consciously and subconsciously, that we don't deserve the things we want.

We must give way to others: put others first, accommodate their wishes and dreams, their physical needs. This is true whether we're

talking about kids, or colleagues, or housemates, or husbands: someone else expresses a whim, and we are supposed to fulfil it. We are supposed to facilitate the lives of the people around us. And if that's at our own expense, so be it. Is it you who remembers the birthdays in your house? Is it you who washes up the mugs in the office kitchen? Is it you who calls the cat-sitter, bleaches the bathroom or picks up the post from the sorting office?

Is it you who writes for the exposure while someone else is making real money? Is it you who stays late to organize the equality committee – or plan the office Christmas do? Is it you who always agrees when someone asks you to do something that really isn't quite in your remit?

Is it you who listens while someone else talks?

Are you tired of living like this?

YOU ARE
WORTHY

This invisible labour exhausts you – and it's supposed to. It's supposed to keep you in your place. It's supposed to stop you reaching your full potential. It grinds you down so that the simple sentence on page 9 feels impossible. *You can have what you want.*

You can have what you want without questioning whether you deserve it; you can have what you want the way it seems that everyone around you can. You are just as worthy of your desires and ambitions as everyone else: as worthy, powerful and complex as anyone else. Why shouldn't your needs be met, too? Why shouldn't you have everything you've ever wanted? What does it feel like to let yourself believe that this is possible?

Because please: believe me.

You, reading this right now, can have what you want.

Make no mistake, it's not that it's going to be easy to make this happen. It's going to take time: I suggest that even reading through this book should take several weeks, making space for each goal and exercise to really sink in.

This isn't magic, not really. It's work, and time, and strength, and dedication. But it is also possible. It is possible to manifest your desires. It is possible to make those dreams a reality, and through the next five chapters of this book we will make that happen. Each chapter centres on a creative visualization or practical exercise to bring us closer to our ideal selves, and ideal lives. As a cleansing moment between each chapter, you'll find a brief pause to centre and ground you.

THE LAW OF
ATTRACTION

This book forms an introduction to one of the most profound concepts known to man: *like calls to like.*

This is the Law of Attraction.

If we think positive thoughts, things are more likely to go well; if we think negative thoughts, things are more likely to feel bad for us. Fairly straightforward, right?

It is, essentially, a kind of applied mindfulness: we need to notice where we are, where we want to be and what has to happen to get us there.

Manifesting first rose to prominence as part of the 19th-century "New Thought" movement, but it's actually much older than that. Think of every culture that believes that to speak the name of evil is to call evil down upon yourself, for example. Think of every prayer that gives prominence to the idea that what we ask for, clearly and articulately, with focus and determination, we shall receive. Our thoughts and feelings have a power that we all instinctively understand, but perhaps underestimate.

And we are *taught* to underestimate our feelings. We are taught from childhood that what we feel, and what we think, are less important than just about every other factor going. We are given limits and boundaries; taught, subconsciously or otherwise, what our lives should look like and the hard edges of our dreams. Our dreams are pushed into shoeboxes, and corralled in service of someone else's systems and success. We are told that to ask for more is greedy, tacky, selfish and unrealistic. Teachers might tell us to aim lower; our families might cut us back down to size or laugh at us

for our ambition. We are told that *feelings aren't facts*; that *facts don't care about our feelings*.

And yet, on reflection, these things are *obviously* not true. Facts respond to feelings all the time. Facts change based on feelings all the time. Just think about it for a moment. Of *course* our feelings can change the facts of our lives: how we react to the world is a direct response to how we feel about the world. How we present to the world changes the way the world presents itself to us: the energy we bring to a situation can change the situation. It can certainly change the responses of those around us.

And all of this is just common sense. It's not magic. It's simply the plain truth. What we think changes the way we act; how we act changes the way we understand; what we understand changes the way we think. We get out, in short, what we put in.

CRUEL QUIRKS OF FATE

This doesn't mean that if you begin to practise manifestation you'll never suffer again. Nothing can change the cruel and random vagaries of fate: you can't unwish cancer, for instance, and nobody can outrun grief forever. It is necessary to address this head on, at the very beginning of this book, because the ideas that power manifestation have so often been used to attack and harm the most vulnerable.

This is notably hard for people with mental health issues like obsessive compulsive disorder or anxiety – who may already struggle with intrusive thoughts – and for those who are going through terrible things. If we wish to benefit from these theories, we have to be willing to tackle the damage they do: if we wish to harness the power of these ideas, we must first *acknowledge* the power they hold for evil as well as good.

Too often manifesting has been turned into yet another instrument of shame and guilt for people already struggling. As in: if you get out what you put in, did people with cancer put cancerous thoughts out into the world? Did they somehow deserve it? Did they deserve to die?

Sometimes we do this to ourselves, too: did I think too much about the bad thing, and then the bad thing happened? Did I call this suffering down on myself?

And the answer to that, of course, is that nobody deserves to suffer; and death is not about our just desserts. Death comes to everyone, sooner or later; and the way death comes is by random accident of our birth and everything that came after. Nobody knows why bad things happen. Nobody knows why terrible things happen to good people; and nobody knows why they happen to bad people either. We just know that they happen every day, and it's heartbreaking.

Anyone who uses the theories of manifesting to make people feel worse is using the theories badly – and will, without a shadow of a doubt, be suffering themselves. If you believe someone died because they didn't believe what you believe, all you're trying to do is protect yourself from fear. You're running away; you're hiding; you're closing off your mind. That's the opposite of everything this stands for, and the opposite of how this all works.

"There is nothing like a dream
to create the future"

Victor Hugo

MANIFESTING
GIVES US HOPE

Manifesting, as we mean it, cannot stop the darkness from falling. But it can help us to turn on the light. Manifesting gives us hope; it gives us power to make small changes that make whatever we're going through better; it gives us a drive to survive, to succeed and to feel joy. It is possible to throw a party on a cancer ward (ask me how I know!) and laugh in the face of impossible danger. It is possible to feel gratitude and gladness at a funeral; and to see the spark of bright hope in Intensive Care. Bring your best self to whatever the universe hands you, and you'll find things are easier. The thing is, practically speaking, *everything* is improved by a good attitude, clear goals, clear actions, solid plans, self-belief, flexibility, focus and open-mindedness.

We use the techniques in this book to open ourselves up to clarity of thought, and clarity of purpose. There is no situation so dire that these twin clarities will not help us through it, and into something like enlightenment. That enlightenment makes life possible, and it makes us powerful. It makes us unafraid, and fear is the mind-killer. Fear holds us back when we most need to leap forward; fear keeps us jumping at shadows, distracted and skittish. It knocks us off our game, and life is hard enough. We need to be on our A-game to get what we want. And I believe that you can do it.

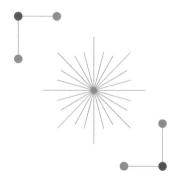

Manifestation gives us a reason to carry on; and it gives us a path to follow when the way is thorny and tangled and lost. Manifestation is applied mindfulness made into a map, plus the willingness to walk the path it shows us. Willingness, in other words, to show up.

We have to show up, for both our present selves – and for our future selves.

The exercises in this book are, in effect, a collaboration between you and your future self: I am simply a conduit between the two of you. (Literally!)

This book is about both of you: about you, now, understanding who she is, and what she wants. What she regrets, and what she's grateful for. What she knows. What she wishes you know. What this powerful, extraordinary person holds dear; what this person, who used to *be* you, can now teach you.

This book is about taking her reality seriously and making that happen. It's about making it happen in our minds so that it can happen in our bodies and in our lives: about making life just a little bit better for the you of tomorrow, about making the path to success as easy as it can possibly be.

So let's go and meet her.

Manifestation gives us a reason to carry on; and it gives us a path to follow when the way is thorny and tangled and lost.

CLARIFICATION MEDITATION

You don't need anything to carry out this meditation, as it's based on an ancient Sanskrit breathing practice called *nadi shodhana*; roughly translated, this means "flow purification". We seek clarity above all things, and in this book we seek in particular clarity of thought. We need to purify the flow of self to let the past go, and the future arrive. This is the channel-clearing breath that lets us get rid of the old, and allow in the new. This is how we throw out the past preconceptions, and welcome in our future self. This breathing exercise is also useful any time we need to wake ourselves up a bit!

Optional extra: some body-safe lavender oil, rubbed onto the thumb and forefinger of each hand, has wonderful healing properties and a strong clarifying scent. Scientifically proven to calm the nervous system, lavender oil relaxes and destresses us for the manifestation work we're about to undertake.

Sit comfortably, with your back as straight as possible. Visualize a clean line from the nape of your neck down to your tailbone.

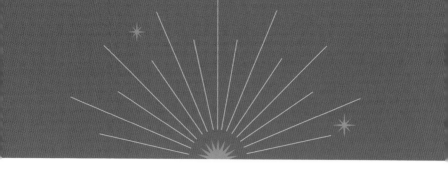

Put your index finger and your middle finger on your forehead, just above your nose. This spot right here is the chakra of the third eye. Opening up, or unblocking, the third eye opens us up to spiritual awakening and clarity. Soften your gaze; or even close your eyes. Inhale the lavender scent, if using.

Cover your right nostril with your thumb.
Close your mouth.

Count in for eight beats, breathing through your open nostril; count out for eight beats through the same open nostril.

Release your right nostril; cover your left nostril with your fourth finger.

Breathe in for eight beats through your open nostril; and out for eight beats through the same open nostril.

Repeat for 12 rounds.

PRACTISING
HAPPINESS

Here's a crucial question: *what makes you happy?*

Now hang on a moment, before you answer that.

For once in this book, don't start daydreaming. This is what happens *before* the daydreaming. This isn't about the imagined future, but the real: the here and now. This is not a hypothetical question. I'm not asking what might make you happy if you had it, or could get it: not a dream, or a wish, but something real and tangible.

I'm asking: *what makes you happy?*

If you can think of something right away, feel free to skip the next bit, and join us at the exercise on the next page.

But if things are pretty grim for you right now, maybe this question makes you feel even worse.

How do you feel about being asked to be happy about your current life? Does it prickle you? Does it disturb you? Does it

make you angry? Maybe you just can't think of anything. Are you, perhaps, angry that the question has been asked? Do you resent the question? Maybe you're thinking: *if I were happy, I wouldn't be reading a book on manifesting...* and that's sort of fair. If this is you: sit with this feeling for a moment, if you don't mind. Your discomfort right now matters. It's important, as *you* are important. Facts aren't feelings, but feelings can be facts. The fact of your discomfort with this question makes you the person this book was written for: the person manifesting was meant for. You're the person with the most to gain from this work.

I'm speaking directly to you, uncomfortable friend, because I don't want you to turn off on the first page of the chapter. You have so much to gain here, and so little to lose – and I know this, because this question stressed you out. The idea of happiness makes you feel prickly. Can you sit for a moment, and wonder why?

FINDING
SOMETHING
WORTHY OF
HAPPINESS

Maybe the answer is because your life completely sucks. Maybe. Maybe there is nothing good or worthwhile in your life at all – perhaps it's a total desert, devoid of anything nice or sparky or interesting. But hear me out here: I just don't think that's true. It might seem like it sometimes, but I think there's something worthy of happiness in every single life in the world. Some person, some object, some sunset, some reflection in a puddle or bus arriving right on time or £2 coffee, that makes your life worth living. Something you noticed. Something you thought.

A ray of sunshine through the slatted blinds; a tiny rainbow prism reflecting off the oxygen monitor; the lavender bush at the end of the street. A cat asleep in a window. I know that, and so do you– because you're still here. And so, I want you to find it. In fact, it's *vital* that you find it. And not just find it, but recognize it.

Your current mood is creating your current mindset, and your current mindset is inextricably linked with your current life. We can't change one without changing the other. And we have to change. That's why we're here: that's the point of manifestation. That's why you came to this book. We can't start visualizing the future without understanding the present: our goals for the future are always motivated by that which we feel we currently lack or built on that which we currently love.

Let's come together now for an exercise in happiness, wherever that question took us initially. Bring it right back to the initial query: *what makes you happy?* Let's start small, and very real.

Where are you right now? You're reading this book, and maybe you're sitting on a bus, or in the kitchen stirring dinner, or even standing in a bookshop wondering whether this book is worth it. I'd like you to ground yourself wherever you are, just for a moment. Settle in to the place

you're in, and – perhaps for the first time, or the first time in a while – I'd like you to really notice it.

If this is hard for you, try engaging all five of your senses. This very common anxiety-reduction technique is amazing for bringing you purposefully and mindfully into the present moment. It works by pulling you away from the over-thinking, intellectual side of the brain – and into the sensations of the physical body. Follow the prompts opposite.

When you've done this, I'd like you to find *one* thing in your present environment that makes you happy. *One tangible, physical thing about this place.* The cup of tea you're holding. The fact you're holding a cup of tea, or maybe it's even your favourite mug. The dinner you're stirring. The music in your headphones. Your new shoes. The fact that you've got a really good pen that isn't even out of ink. Nice glasses; a vase of flowers; the sound of rain on the roof. I believe you can do this, even if the rest of everything sucks.

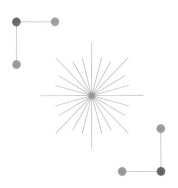

*

Breathe deep, and find:

Five things you can see

Four things you can hear

Three things you can feel

Two things you can smell

One thing you can taste

*

HAPPINESS
LIST

I'd like you to take your Manifestation Journal (see pages 11–12), and on the first page I'd like you to write a sentence about this thing that makes you happy.

It can just be: *This mug of tea makes me so happy.*

Then, try expanding it out: *I love having tea in this mug, because it was a gift from my daughter.*

And once more: *This very ugly Santa Claus mug makes me happy, because it makes me think about the sweet image of my little daughter choosing it for me in the Christmas All Year Round shop on her school trip.*

Or perhaps:

I love the sound of the rain on the roof.

I love the sound of the rain on the roof because I'm glad I'm not outside.

I love the sound of the rain on the roof because it makes me grateful for my home, and all the work I have put in to get here.

Or perhaps:

It makes me happy that this pen isn't out of ink.

It makes me happy that this pen isn't out of ink because usually my colleagues take all the good pens.

It makes me happy that this pen isn't out of ink because someone thought of me and left me this one, which is my favourite; or even: It makes me happy that this pen isn't out of ink because I got up early this morning and went to the shop to buy one that I really love.

Do you notice something about what happens when we expand out the things that make us happy? Yep: we find more things that make

Being happy is an exercise, and it improves every time you do it.

us happy. We find out more about the things that make us happy, and sometimes even how we got to be happy in the first place. Let's look at those three examples: a mug of tea, rain on the roof and a pen that works. They are such small, everyday things, but they all show us so much more.

They show us pride in a daughter's generosity; pride in our own hard work; and pride in our friends or

our own sense of self-worth. Or maybe: love of our family; love of our home; and love of self. The small things *are* the big things. Time to stand in a bookshop and choose a book is a luxury; money and ease of ordering a book online are luxuries; a moment in the library is a luxury. All of them can make us happy, and all of them spiral outward to show us so many more things that make life worth living.

And they show us, too, that happiness is a practice.

Like everything else worth doing, being happy is an exercise, and it improves every time you do it. Actively looking for happiness is a choice and one that begins, perhaps, right here. When we find one thing to be happy about, we can always find more.

FULL BODY SCAN

Lie comfortably on your bed or sofa, and take a few deep breaths. Inhale through the nose, and exhale fully through the mouth. Feel the breath in your nostrils, your throat and in your lungs. If you can, try to flare your ribs and fill your diaphragm with air. Feel the air inflating; and then exhale, fully and totally, through the mouth. Feel yourself rise, and fall. Close your eyes, if you can, or soften your gaze as much as possible.

Your attention should be fully on the breath, but don't worry if your mind drifts away. You are complete; you are correct and complete as you are. Accept yourself.

This is a mindfulness exercise, so just gently bring your attention back to the breath. The breath is an anchor here, and it's going to keep us where we need to be. Trust that it will keep you where you need to be.

Breathe in, breathe out. When you feel fully present in the stream of breath, and the rise and fall of your lungs, I'd like you to bring your attention to your physical form. How does your body feel? How does the bed or sofa feel, supporting your body? Where is your body touching the softness, and how is the softness holding you up?

You're allowed to feel silly doing this, but you're also allowed to take yourself seriously here. You're allowed to take this time for yourself. Focus on the places your body touches the bed; focus on the places your body touches itself.

And then we draw this attention to a singular point: your little toes. There they are. Have you ever noticed them before, excepting blisters? Probably not. Notice them now, and visualize them lit with a warm glow. Switch on the light in your little toes. Now move that light. Picture it spreading, and with the light your attention: your toes, one by one; the arches and soles of your feet; your heels. The light moves into your ankles, and so on, slowly up the legs: ankles to calves, calves to knees, knees to thighs, thighs to hips. Is there pain anywhere? Any tension? Any pressure? Find the sensation, or lack of sensation. Breathe deeply, and keep moving that light, very slowly, with the breath.

Bring the light through the pelvis, and the sitting bones, and bring it up, up the spine. The breath moves the spine and the belly and the chest, and the warm light moves with it. Breathe in, breathe out. Focus your attention on the warm

light; if it wanders, use the breath as an anchor. Feel free to come back to the breath for as long as you like.

The light, warm and loving, fills your chest and shoulders. Your upper arms, your triceps, your elbows: all filled with light. Hands, fingers, fingernails and fingertips: all blessed by light and breath. Love yourself; love every part of yourself; and every sensation. Think: thank you, body. Love your body. Love yourself. Love the light as it moves.

Breathe in, breathe out. Move your attention back through the fingers, into the hands, the light shining through every vein and tendon. The arms become the shoulders become the neck, and move your attention and that warm, loving light into your face and mind. Neck, throat, chin, cheeks; the mouth, nose, eyes, ears and scalp. Your beautiful brain that makes everything work. Touch it with light; love it; thank it. Your memories. Your emotions. Your feelings right now. Breathe in. Breathe out. Give thanks and be blessed with your own loving light.

"Most people are about as happy
as they make up their mind to be."

✳

Abraham Lincoln

EMBRACING THE PRESENT

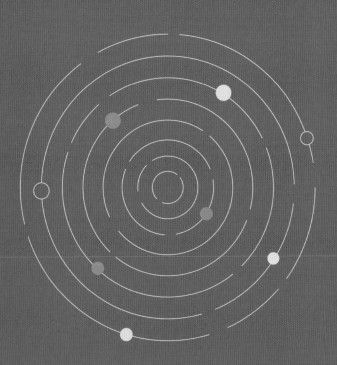

Let's try another question for the here and now: *what are you thankful for?*

Gratitude is not the same as happiness; it has, perhaps, a symbiotic relationship with happiness. As our happiness grows, so too must our gratitude; but as our gratitude grows, science shows, so too does our happiness.

It is this latter fact that is so remarkable. Being happy makes us grateful, of course – but being grateful makes us happy. The act of being thankful for something gives us permission, and perhaps a reminder, to be happy about it. And not just that. When we are grateful for one thing, we open our hearts to be grateful for more; the more gratitude we feel, the happier we are – and the better our physical and mental health overall. Studies have shown – reported by institutions as widely renowned as Berkeley and Harvard – that gratitude is key to almost everything good in life. Subjects in gratitude studies, almost universally, report increased happiness in everything: careers, families, homes and selves. By putting gratitude at the centre of our lives, we promote general optimism, better relationships and increased empathy. Empathy, of course, creates connection; and it's connection that makes the world turn in our favour.

And these factors are crucial to successful manifestation. Our mental state has everything to do with the way we walk through life, and people who walk through life with a strongly positive mental attitude will find things are easier. Not only that, but gratitude empowers us to understand how much has been given to us: when we recognize how much has been given to us, we recognize how worthy we are of grace, of love, of kindness and of luck. When we feel

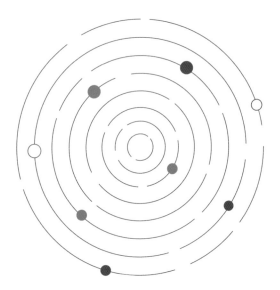

worthy, we are ready to receive whatever the world can give us.

Gratitude shakes off those mental blocks that hold us back: it shakes down the part of us that says we don't deserve love, and laughs at it. Look at everything we have! Look how lucky we are! It opens up our hearts to abundance and, when we look on the world with abundance, that is what comes to us. We get

out what we put in, remember, and if we project confidence and abundance that is what we will find.

This is true, incidentally, even if we don't exactly feel it. "Fake it 'til you make it" is not a notably beautiful slogan, but it turns out to be just a little bit correct: the more you smile, according to one collation study in 2019, the happier you feel. The more you frown, the sadder you feel. The more you scowl, the angrier you feel. This research, from the University of Tennessee, collated over 130 separate studies from different scholars – so there must be something to it. Our own facial expressions are holding us back. Our own *perceptions* of our negativity only create more negativity – so we have to try, by any means possible, to make ourselves smile.

✦

Gratitude shakes off those mental blocks that hold us back: it shakes down the part of us that says we don't deserve love, and laughs at it.

✦

GRATITUDE LIST

So let's begin: take your Journal, and turn to a fresh
double page.

Working quickly – don't overthink it! – let's dedicate
these pages to gratitude.

What are you grateful for?

(If you're stuck, your Happiness List on page 38
might help as a jumping-off point.)

We are going to fill this page with gratitude. Yes: fill it.
Do you find this daunting? You might. But I promise you,
you're going to be able to do it. The first thing is always
the hardest, but gratitude has a snowball effect. You will
be able to fill this page with things you're grateful for.
Here's some fun categories to get you started…

Friends	Accomplishments	Health
Family	Food	Time
Partner	Water	Warmth
Career	Home	Senses

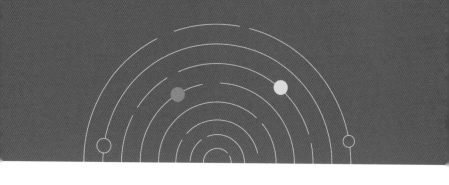

Joys	Money	...a cool drink
Passions	Life	...a cosy blanket
Projects	Freedom	...a good book
Skills	Stories	...a soft sweater
Music	Dreams	...clean sheets
Art	Hopes	...coffee
Nature	Fears(!)	...chocolate
Love	...and...	...house plants
Sex	...a hot bath	...yourself

If you have washi tape, a fun thing to do is to write each gratitude on a strip of tape, and stick them down into your Journal. It can help you to really see the depth and magnitude of your gratitude, especially as they build up over time – because, trust me, we will be coming back to this page.

Gratitude has both an immediate and a long-term effect on our positive mental health. It has what some manifesting experts call a "compound" effect: the more we practise it, the deeper the benefits become. We get better at it, actually – just like with happiness. This page, by the time we finish the Journal, will be weighty with thankfulness: a tangible reminder of why we do this.

WRITE
ABOUT IT

It's not just being grateful that helps – it's also the act of writing about it. In fact, it's mainly the act of writing about it. A 2018 Berkeley study brought 300 people together, each suffering from a mental or physical health condition, to consider how gratitude might help them with their existing troubles. The researchers gave each participant psychotherapy, but otherwise split the group into three: one, the control team, had only the psychotherapy; the second was given psychotherapy, and asked to write about their feelings on the subject; and the third group was given psychotherapy and asked to write specifically about gratitude. In fact, they were asked to write letters to someone or something – a different thing each day – expressing their thankfulness and love.

Would it surprise you to learn that this third group reported the greatest improvement in wellbeing? They slept better; they felt less pain; they felt better in themselves. When we manifest our gratitude, the universe rewards us for what we put in. They didn't even have to send the letters to anyone. Just the act of writing helped. They focused on the positive; they expressed their love; they were – genuinely– just a little bit *healed* by it.

Manifestation is as much about healing as it is anything else: we must work to heal past hurt, and past trauma, in order to move away from our negative self-belief. Gratitude is our number one weapon against our preconceived ideas of our own suffering. Remember that Berkeley study? The researchers took all the writings produced, and compared those of Group Three to those of

Group Two. They found that Group Three, the gratitude group, used significantly more positive words and significantly fewer negative words. They deduced that it was exactly this – the *lack* of negativity – that had created such a boost in the participants' wellbeing. They shed negative beliefs; they shed pain ; and they were better able to imagine their lives going forward.

The act of "creatively imagining" gratitude for the present revealed the possibility of the same for the future. The physical commitment to writing helps us artistically and emotionally rewrite the story we are living in – and that is manifestation in a nutshell.

We have to make this kind of gratitude practice part of our daily routines, not just a one-off experiment.

Remember the washi tape in the Journal exercise? Part of what is so wonderful about an ongoing

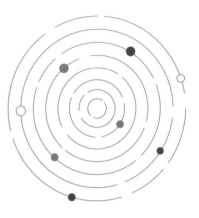

gratitude practice is that we get to see and feel the "gratitude" build up: we have something solid to support our belief that we are worthy of abundance, and worthy of love. Plus, we have something to dip back into on dark days: a very real well of joy and strength to tide us through the stress and fear. It can be hard to fight our way through our own minds to find some glint of light, so if we have something tangible in our Journal (or on the mantelpiece...) to lean on, it can make all the difference. And we are all about making that difference for ourselves, right?

So there are two ways to do this. The first continues from the Journal exercise we've just done, but the second I strongly recommend if the Journal exercise felt totally overwhelming. If you didn't manage to get on with that exercise, try this...

The physical commitment to writing helps us artistically and emotionally rewrite the story we are living in – and that is manifestation in a nutshell.

THE GRATITUDE JAR

A nice thing about this exercise is that it can be a two –
(or more!) player game.

Much of manifesting is, by nature, quite a solitary activity...
and yet involving other people (particularly those you hope
to bring along on your journey) can be a huge help. It can
be profoundly motivational to talk about your quest to feel
better, and having someone else join in can keep you both
going on days that feel hard. It's a sweet activity to do with
a partner, and – unlike a lot of the exercises in this book
– is highly recommended for kids. It makes a wonderful
introduction to the world of manifesting!

The Gratitude Jar is very simple: you take a glass jar, and
put it somewhere you can see it. Maybe you paint the jar
with poster paint or acrylic to make it beautiful; maybe you
just write THE GRATITUDE JAR on it in Sharpie; maybe
you wrap it around in washi tape. Maybe you leave it plain.
It's a good idea to be mindful about what you're doing:
make sure it feels special. Don't leave the pickle label on!
(If you are involving children in this activity, this is a great
way to make them feel involved with the project from
the start.)

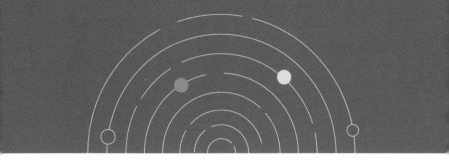

You'll then need either some plain wooden ice lolly sticks, or a stack of strips of paper. The paper can be folded for privacy, but the ice lolly sticks are satisfying to thumb through: a Rolodex of thankfulness.

Every day, you take a slip of paper, or ice lolly stick, and write on it one thing you're grateful for. Just one. No bother. Drop it into the jar, and go about your day. Make it part of your routine, perhaps first thing in the morning or last thing before bed.

A flash of gratitude. A tiny prayer to the places and people and things that you love.

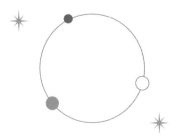

THE GRATITUDE JOURNAL

This works much the same as the Gratitude Jar on page, except that a) it's in your Journal, so you have more space to be creative and b) you're going to write down three things instead of one.

And you're going to make this into a little ritual, too. This one, being more private, feels like something to do last thing at night: make yourself a herbal tea, light a candle and set a timer for five minutes. This isn't self-indulgence: it's actually a huge part of why it works. You have to *want* to be happy for happiness to come to you. (Read that again, if it needs saying twice. It feels surprisingly revolutionary to just admit it.)

Take a deep breath: breathe in love, breathe in truth, breathe in peace. Breathe in everything you're grateful for, along with the clean air and space and time to do this in. Be aware of how lucky you are, as you write. Everything in this moment is a gift; that, as they say, is why they call it the present.

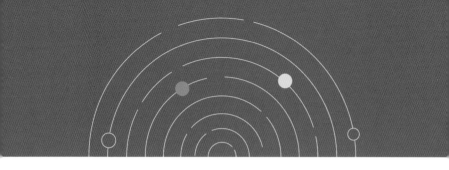

Open your Journal, thumb through the Happiness List on page 38 and the Gratitude List on pages 50-51. Take your pen, and write.

Each night, take five minutes to do this. After a week, check in with yourself. How is this working for you? How do you feel? How about after a month? A year?

We're not looking for quick fixes, here. We're looking to cultivate a headspace where the world is welcome. We're looking to change the way we respond to the world; and what the world brings to us. We are signifying our openness to abundance: to joy.

These practices are drawn from gratitude studies, of course – not from manifestation techniques, which are much less frequently studied. But gratitude *is* manifestation; mindfulness *is* manifestation. The power of the mind to heal itself is the same power we harness to shape a life that works for us. When we write about our gratitude, we make ourselves more grateful. When we write about our happiness, we make ourselves happier. We make the reality we want to live in.

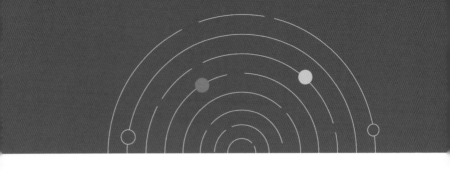

This is literally true: couples, for instance, who take the time to be grateful for their partner are reputedly better able to communicate problems with that partner. They are able to articulate concerns and request changes – without feeling like the sky is going to fall in. Couples able to articulate what they love about their partner are much more secure in their relationship; and that security translates to an increased ability to be flexible, change, and in turn ask for change.

We need that security; we need that flexibility and, above all, we need that change. We have come to this place to change together: to become that future self we've dreamed of meeting.

And in this wealth of love, perhaps, we are almost ready.

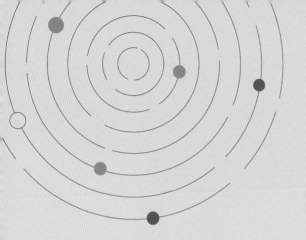

Grant me the serenity to accept
the things I cannot change,
courage to change the things I can,
and wisdom to know the difference.

✳

Serenity Prayer

MEETING THE FUTURE

Imagine you're in a café.

It's the distant future, so you can imagine it as futuristically as you like. Perhaps you are on the Moon colony. Silver spacesuits, if that's what floats your boat. Everyone sipping protein shakes from foil packets. You have lived a full and rich life, and this is just the latest hub of it.

Really picture it; add as much colour and character to it as you can. Imagine what you can see; what you can smell; hear; taste. A cool breeze. The space café is busy.

(This isn't for nothing: creative imagining takes work and practice, like everything else. This little game is silly, but actually pretty helpful: it gives us a framework in which to exercise imagination. It gives us a space to play in, and toys to play with: spacesuits, a moon café, a foil-packet protein shake. You see, the better we get at this kind

of imagining, the easier it will be to manifest our own will when the time comes.)

So you're sitting there, nibbling your freeze-dried astro-brunch, when you hear your name somewhere in the hubbub of conversation. The people at the next table are talking about you.

The eavesdropper's exercise is one of our most useful visualization tools for helping us to embody our future selves.

They're really getting into it: they don't know you're here. Perhaps you are hidden by a large space pot plant, or moon door. They're talking about your long, rich, full life; the things you've done; how easy you made it look. How you succeeded where so many others had failed. What an inspiration you are. What a life you've led (first on Earth, and now – obviously, keep up – here on the Moon). The achievements, the hurdles and, above all, your character.

"Obviously, they gave it everything," one says. "They never gave in."

"They worked so hard for it all, that's true," says the other. Then she adds – *what?*

What would you like her to say next?

What exactly do you want her to have known about you?

What would you most want to overhear about yourself?

Of course, the space scene is sort of funny – but this exercise, known as the Eavesdropper's Exercise – is actually pretty serious. It's one of our most useful visualization tools for helping us to embody our future selves. If someone were to talk about your future self, what would you like them to say?

Imagine opening up the newspaper one morning, and seeing your own picture there. Then imagine realizing that it's in the Obituaries section. *Then* imagine realizing that there's a headline over your picture, at the top of your obituary, and the headline reads: *The Merchant of Death is Dead.*

THE MERCHANT OF DEATH IS DEAD

You look at the text of the obituary. You read: "Mr Nobel, who devoted his life to finding new ways to kill people..."

This is the headline that greeted Alfred Nobel one morning over breakfast in 1888. His brother had died, and the papers had somehow got the wrong end of the stick and published the wrong obituary. This was Alfred's own obituary, and it was damning. Alfred Nobel was an inventor, and he had invented – among other lethal creations – dynamite. He had taken his dynamite money, and poured it into arms manufacturing: steel, cannons, a new kind of smokeless explosive. And this, then, was his legacy.

Shaken, Alfred decided he could not live with this – and dedicated the rest of his life, and almost his entire fortune, to establishing the Nobel Prizes. Among them, of course, was the Nobel Peace Prize. He wanted to be different. He wanted to change the way he was thought of, and change his memory. The obituary he had imagined for himself turned out to be different from the obituary the world had for him – and being forced to recognize that gave him the power to recognize, too, where his life would have to change. Let's consider now the following questions.

*What would you want your
obituary to say?
And, if you died tomorrow, what
would your obituary say?*

Morbid? Maybe. But a vital
exercise in understanding
how far you have to go to reach
your goals, and in
what direction.

*What would your headline be now?
What would you like it to be?
And what has to change for you to
get what you want?*

In other words:

What are your values?

**Values are your
standards of
behaviour; the
guiding principles
that govern your
actions.**

CORE VALUES

The word "values" is a tricky one: it can have a kind of slippery quality to it that makes it hard to pin down. For us, though, we're going to define "personal values" as the qualities we respect in ourselves and in others: the qualities that make a "good" person rather than a "bad" person.

(Dividing people up into "good" and "bad" is also a bit slippery, but go with it. Let's pretend we're living in a world where everything is that simple.)

So these are your standards of behaviour; the guiding principles that govern your actions. These values are what you cherish in others, and try to live up to yourself – or, perhaps, the other way round. When we define our values, we get to define the parameters of a good life. We can't set goals unless we know what values are driving those goals, and we certainly can't

manifest anything unless we know why we want it.

"I want to get rich" isn't a motivational thought; "I want to buy my mother a house so she can end her days in security and comfort" is specific, helpful and an active driver in our success.

If we expand that out still further, to our core values – say, "I want to look after my mother just as she looked after me, and loyalty and care are two things that I value highly" – we can tell a story about ourselves that can shape us into a better person.

A person who knows their core values is a person who knows herself; a person who lives up to her core values is a person who loves herself; a person who loves herself is self-sufficient, driven, motivated, capable and competent. And that person is someone who achieves. That person is someone who gets stuff done: gets what they want.

CORE VALUE CLOUD

Grab your Journal, now, and we're going to make a word cloud of our core values.

Look back over the things you're grateful for, and in particular look back at the Happiness List on page 38. What do those moments of happiness embody? What values are represented in the things that make us happy, and the things for which we're grateful? What values do we have that have made those things happen? How did we achieve those things?

Here's some ideas to get you started. What resonates with you here? What has brought you happiness up to this point? What has brought you gratitude? Which words below might you live by?

Adaptability	Frugality	Personal growth
Altruism	Generosity	Self-reliance
Appreciation	Gentleness	Self-respect
Assertiveness	Gratitude	Selflessness
Attentiveness	Honesty	Spirituality
Calmness	Hope	Supportive
Care	Humility	Sustainability
Compassion	Improvement	Thoughtfulness
Courage	Integrity	Tolerance
Dependability	Intellect	Toughness
Determination	Kindness	Trustworthiness
Empathy	Laughter	Uniqueness
Equanimity	Loyalty	Wellbeing
Family	Open-mindedness	
Flexibility	Patience	

What do you want more of? What do you want to
hear about yourself in a space café? What do you
want to read about yourself in your own obituary?

LOOKING
FORWARD

This chapter has, so far, been set in the distant future. We've talked about your life at your life's close, and your life in the spacesuit-wearing Moon Unit. But what of everything between now and then? Why have we skipped over that part?

Well, we've skipped that part until now because that part is the hardest. If we give ourselves some distance – say, the distance between here and the Moon, or the distance between life and death – it's easier to imagine the perfect, values-led self we long to be. That person can be as flawless as we like; the gulf is so huge that our self-imaginings aren't constrained by any doubt or fear. We don't have to be "realistic" about it, when we imagine ourselves being praised in space.

You see, when we try to be "realistic" about what we can achieve, often what that really means is that we begin by imposing limits on ourselves. We begin by thinking of all the things we could never do, or never make ourselves do. So why not start at the other end? Why not start in a starry world where we *did* make everything happen, just the way we've always dreamed, and work back from there?

If we know where we want to end up, and we know where we are now, we can begin to make a map of what the journey will look like. Once we have a rough shape of the journey, we can begin to plot our waypoints. These waypoints are the successes we hope to achieve, and will achieve, given work and time and luck: waypoints at 20 years, 10 years, 5 years, 1 year from now.

Waypoints that, in the mind of the elderly person in the space café, are beautiful memories on her journey. I'd like us to sit with that future self now for a little while.

Really picture what it feels like to be her: you could try the Five Senses exercise on pages 36-37, in an imaginative way, to become your future self.

I'd like us to know what she knows, see what she sees, remember what she remembers. Remember when she was your age; remember when she was a year older than you; remember when she was five years older than you, ten years older than you, twenty years older than you.

Try thinking: *I remember when...*

What comes to mind? What achievements, goals, successes and beautiful moments does she remember, and do you imagine? What would you like her to remember? The sounds of the space café fall away for her, and she remembers her life, that will be your life. What is she daydreaming about? What do you daydream about? Find your shared dreams, held tight by your shared values, and remember those moments as if you have already lived them...

You may even want to journal about these moments. Some people find a "Journal Entry from the Future Self" to be highly motivating. Date the page a year from now, and let yourself write as if everything you hope for has already happened.

Dear Diary, what a year!

We don't stop playing because we grow old;
we grow old because we stop playing.

George Bernard Shaw

NOURISHING THE PAST

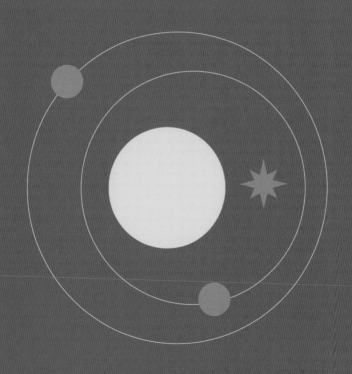

This chapter is a playground. Welcome.

We have learned much, in the previous three chapters: our core values, our sacred gratitudes, our present happinesses. We have met our future self, as we hope she will be, and we have sat in our current lives, and found much to be thankful for within them. We know so much, now. We know who we are; we know who we would like to be.

So here's a question for you:

What *don't* you know?

We think we know what we want, and maybe we do... but what about everything else? What about the things we have never even thought to consider? What is our certainty, or newfound certainty, shutting out? What are our preconceived ideas of success hiding from us?

Keep this question at the forefront of your mind as we move through this chapter, and work together to centre playful creativity in your life. This is a chapter of surprise, of sparkle: a chapter based on movement, action and joy. This is, you might say, a sacred space for electricity and creativity and chaos. Who knows what you might discover? What might you find within yourself, if you allow yourself to step outside your rigid boundaries of self?

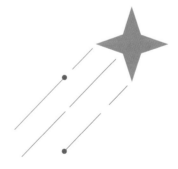

You're going to have to get comfortable with making mistakes, with things being imperfect and messy and silly.

I'm going to insist, in this chapter, that you really commit to the bit. Even – especially – if you don't think it's within your skill set. Even if you're not "creative". Even if you're not "artsy". This chapter is for you: the grown-up who has forgotten how to invent things.

If you struggled with the imaginative space café scene in the previous chapter, this one is for you. Go with it, please. Give in.

This chapter is also specifically for the perfectionists: for everyone who wants things to look exactly right, and for everyone who struggles with making mistakes. You're going to have to get comfortable with mistakes, here: with things being imperfect and messy and silly. You're going to get comfortable with scissors and glue and cutting and sticking and drawing. Maybe even a gel pen.

NOURISHING OUR INNER CHILD

You see, if we have embraced the present, and embraced the future, we have also to embrace the past: our child-self must be given space to flourish and the tools to express. This is especially true if you were never given this time back then.

Everyone has an inner child, and she must be allowed to play. She needs love; she needs care; she needs encouragement and time and affection. An inner child is part

of the subconscious that remains little and needy; and too often in adult life she gets forgotten and ignored. Do you ever feel yourself losing your temper, or tears forming in your eyes when you feel left out, or a rush of stupid joy when you smell toffee apples or stamp through fallen leaves? Do you ever feel anxious even though there's no rational reason to do so? Do you ever find yourself feeling clingy or desperate or fearful, even when you know you should let go and step out into the world? That's your inner child. Sometimes, she's scared because she's a kid. Sometimes, she's scared because she's stuck in the past, and she can't get past it. Often, we don't know how to let our inner child express her feelings; and so she stays down there in the dark, not really understanding, not really being able to move forward. It's lonely, in your subconscious. She doesn't understand the adult world you live in. If you had a hard childhood – felt bullied or forgotten – she doesn't know that things have changed. She acts deep down; makes you grab onto things and not let go; makes you grab onto old ideas and old patterns because there's a certain kind of safety in there.

To move forward, we have to parent that inner child. We have to look after the smallest, most vulnerable parts of ourselves with tenderness and wisdom; we have to bring to our deepest psyche the love we would show a hurt and hopeful child. We have to care for ourselves; we have to love ourselves inwardly, thoroughly, respectfully. If we don't, she's going to stay in the dark– and no amount of external validation can get through. If we don't love ourselves, we can't go on. We manifest nothing when the inner child is holding us to ransom. What does she need? What does she want?

This is not an exercise, because it can't be practised on demand, but the next time you feel these immature, desperate emotions – stop for a moment. Pretend you're caring for a child having a tantrum. Ask your inner self: *Hey, buddy, what do we need? What do you need right now?* Speak to yourself with compassion. Speak to yourself with care; give yourself boundaries; give yourself clear instructions. Take your inner child somewhere safe; explain carefully what needs to happen. Love her. Nourish her. Let her play.

Manifesting can easily slip into the world of "toxic positivity", and this is one way we counter that: by letting the inner child express herself through play. And by play I mean that we let the inner child feel joy; we let her do things just because. A walk in the park. An afternoon drawing. A lunchtime dance party. Play enhances so much about our life: it gives us a much-needed endorphins boost, it stimulates the mind and sparks creativity. What don't we know? What might play give us? What might we find out if we do things just for the hell of them?

We have to look after the smallest, most vulnerable parts of ourselves with tenderness and wisdom.

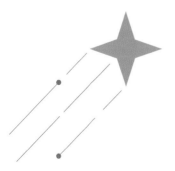

PLAY
MAKES OUR
CONNECTIONS
STRONGER

In your Journal, now, let's touch base with that child self. **What did you love to do? What made you happy then? What games did you play? How did you play?**

Let's consider how we can absorb those joys into part of our adult daily life.

You probably loved playing with your friends: do you make enough time for friendship in your life now? Could you prioritize friendship more? Could you take a couple of hours a week to go dancing with a pal, or sit down for a coffee and a gossip? You could even get stuck into a board game or video game, or go for a run through the park. You could take a new class, or join a meet-up group for a hobby you've always wanted to try. Play helps us build those social connections like nothing else; and social connections are what keep us connected to the world.

Play strengthens our existing connections, and helps us establish more. It allows us to resolve conflict, and feel excited about things again. (After all, what's flirting if not a kind of play?) It gives us a space to replenish our creativity, and consider things from new angles – and new perspectives. New people give us new perspectives, and new perspectives open up new doors.

We open up avenues to the universe, and through those avenues our dreams come true. You never know when that person you meet at a yoga class might be the person you fall in love with; you never know when the person you volunteer with at the community library might have just the job opportunity you've been looking for all this time. The more we reach out to people, the more the world reaches out to us. The more we can give, the more we can get – and, luckily for us, it's a self-perpetuating cycle.

The more creative, energized and nourished we are, the more we are able to put that energy out into the universe; and the more it returns to us. This is at the heart of manifesting: you get out what you put in. Like attracts like. Love attracts love. Spark attracts spark.

So let's reignite the spark. If once you loved making things, could you make things again? If you loved baking cupcakes, could you come home from work tonight and bake? Could you sit down and draw? Could you swing on the swings in the park, play with a friend's dog, play dress-up with all the prettiest things in your closet? What did Little You think your adult self would be? What did you dream of? What did you want?

Yes – it's time to ask these questions:

What is it that you want?

What would make you happier?

What is it that you desire?

What are you hoping to manifest?

When you were a kid, did you ever go through a catalogue with a pen and/or scissors? Do you remember how you would mark or cut out everything you wanted? Maybe you even stuck it all together to make a kind of dream house.

MAKING A
VISION BOARD

This next exercise is a grown-up's dream house. It's called
a vision board, and it's one of the most famous and useful
tools in all manifesting. You can do this in your Journal,
but you can also do this on posterboard or a pinboard and
display it somewhere prominently.

The idea is to make a visual, tangible representation of
your goals and hopes. It's also meant to spark ideas: to play
with the idea of desire and dreams, to allow us to make
physical metaphors of everything we hope to achieve.

We use the creative spirit of the past self, the child, to
carry the dreams of the present self into the reality of
the future self.

Gather together sharp scissors, a stack of old magazines
and newspapers, some good glue and washi tape, and
either your Journal or a board.

Cork boards are good because they can be updated regularly and prominently displayed; but a Journal has benefits, too, like being physically connected to your lists of happiness and gratitude, your future and your past.

Some people also may choose to print images off the internet - perhaps using Pinterest or Instagram for inspiration. This is fine, but I'd strongly recommend you do actually make something tangible. A digital board can be beautiful, but that connection you get from handmaking something can't be faked: the truth forged by your physical act of cutting and sticking and creation is much more important than how the thing actually looks. You will be surprised by your work; you will find things you never knew to look for.

We're going to go through the newspapers and magazines to find things that embody our dreams and goals: any powerful words, any beautiful pictures, even symbols. Start with the big picture, if the specifics don't jump out at you right away: a deserted beach to symbolize peace, a sparkling diamond to symbolize wealth, a roaring fire in a cosy hearth to symbolize safety.

Cut first, and stick later: be abundant in what you take and what you permit yourself to want. Make a stack of images and words that you feel drawn to, and try not to limit yourself. Let that child play.

Bring your best self. Bring your sparkiest, most creative ideas. Bring feathers, beads, ribbon – anything at all that you find beautiful that sums you up, your future self up. Indulge your inner child's wish for things to be pretty.

A tip: if you want your adult self to believe it's pretty too, try choosing images mostly from a similar colour palette. You can also stick each image and word onto a sheet of plain paper, and then cutting neatly around the edges to create a standard border – to give the board a feeling of cohesiveness. Washi tape, too, can act as a great border between images. This might seem frivolous, but it's really not: indulge that inner-child need for lovely things at the same time as your outer adult's need for aesthetic joy. You are allowed beauty. You are allowed pleasure. You deserve joy. You have to want to look at this: you have to want to keep this in your line of sight, and to see it every day as a motivational tool.

This board is a treasure chest of your hopes: make it lovely,
be bold, be smart. This is not a place for negativity. This is
not a place to decide what you *don't* want. This is a place
to bring your hope. Positive vibes only, as they say. Positive
Mental Attitude. This is manifesting, right here: devoting
time and energy to making the future you want out of the
things you already have in your hand. This is work, and
you're doing it. You are literally making it happen. And be
prepared – always be prepared – to surprise yourself.

What do you want?

What goals have emerged from this exercise?

What's made you happy?

What do you want more of?

What's on this board that isn't in your life?

What do you want?

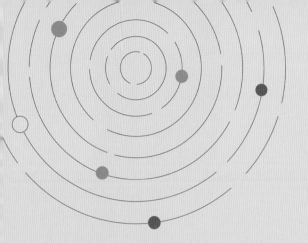

Once you make a decision,
the universe conspires
to make it happen.

Ralph Waldo Emerson

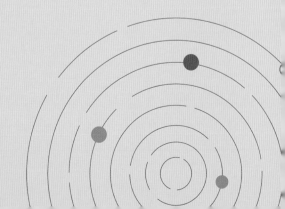

CREATING THE PLAN

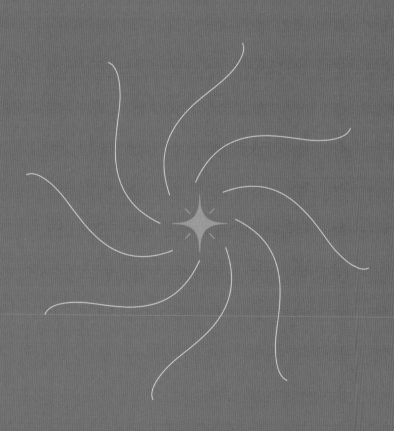

Hold your Journal in your hand. Feel the weight of it.

We bring together in this Journal our values, our vision board, and our tallies of our present happiness and gratitude; we unite our past, present and future selves in pursuit of something greater. We have touched the vast, like our words to live by, and the tiny, like an ugly mug. We have talked about the sublime, the silly, the pure and the playful – and now it's time to bring all this into one single goal.

Quite literally, because now is the time to set our *actual*, concrete goals – and the time to achieve them.

You can have what you want, if you can say what you want. I believe that, if you've worked your way through this book, you're ready to put those things into words and the words on the page. Enough talking from me; and enough thinking about the past. It's time to get to work. It's time to set our goals.

Take your Journal. Take a fresh page. And write down three factual, practical goals. Draw on everything we've learned so far: everything that makes you happy, everything that you're grateful for, all your values.

Relate each goal back to those values, if you can: remember, not just "I want to be rich", but "I want enough money to build security for my family". Be confident. Be specific. Be precise. Ask, and it shall be granted to you.

Start each with: *I want...* Now, for each of these goals, I want you to reword it. Reword it as if it's not a request, but a certainty. *I will...*

And a third time, reword it. This time, reword each goal as if it's already happened, and happened to you. Speak as your future self, confident and secure. *I am...*

FIVE-FIVE-FIVE
AND
THREE-SIX-NINE

A crucial part of manifestation is in the act of writing, as we've already learned - but it's about to kick up a notch. It is very simple: we write out our goal daily. In doing so, we focus the mind and the universe on achieving that goal. Our body becomes a vehicle for achieving that goal, and our heart becomes open to it. Our mind becomes dedicated to the goal, almost as if in a meditation.

You can do this in the five-five-five method, or the newly popular three-six-nine: it's completely up to you. They both work exactly the same: first thing in the morning, some time in the afternoon and last thing at night, you write out your goals. You write, and keep writing, until the goal is achieved. Some people like to check in after a symbolic number of days - for instance, five days, or five weeks, from the start of writing-but I don't like putting this kind of deadline on the universe. It provides. You're doing your best; accept that the universe may well be doing hers.

You write them out right here, in the Journal. Obviously, you can

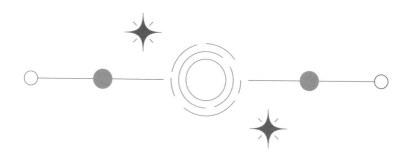

do this either five times each time, or three times in the morning, six times at lunchtime and nine before bed. It doesn't matter which you're drawn to. Some people love the symmetry of five-five-five; others prefer the gradual climb of three-six-nine.

Many people favour the three-six-nine technique because it hands over the work to our subconscious mind. You see, our conscious mind might throw up all kinds of obstacles in the way of these goals – but our dreaming mind has no such hang ups. If our last thoughts before sleep are of what we hope to achieve, our dreams can turn over the problem and perhaps find us solutions. Some people even tuck the Journal under their pillow. We must live with our goals: we must make them the centre of our being.

FOCUS WHEEL

Let us see what our lives look like when reconfigured around our goals. This exercise is a focus wheel, adapted from a classic manifestation worksheet – and it allows us to figure out what exactly we need to do to give the universe the best chance of helping us out.

Remember, *like calls to like*: we want to bring our own spiritual "vibration" as closely in line with the "vibrations" of our goal as possible. We want to make our life and home a space in which all our values align.

Take your Journal, and draw a large circle that almost touches the edges of the paper. You probably want to do this on a double-page spread – you may even want to use a compass.

Next, inside the big circle draw a smaller circle, and inside that smaller circle, a smaller circle still. Don't write anything in the inner circle yet, but divide both the middle and outer "ring" into 12 equal parts.

We're going to make one of these focus wheels for each of our three goals.

It should look something like this. Don't worry about the words yet – we're getting to that.

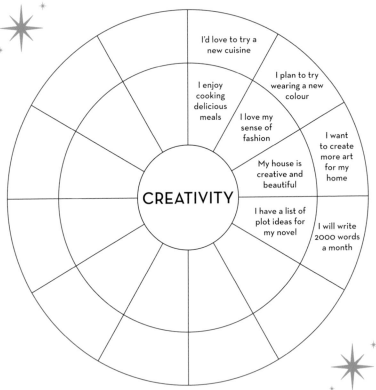

CREATIVITY

I'd love to try a new cuisine

I plan to try wearing a new colour

I enjoy cooking delicious meals

I love my sense of fashion

I want to create more art for my home

My house is creative and beautiful

I have a list of plot ideas for my novel

I will write 2000 words a month

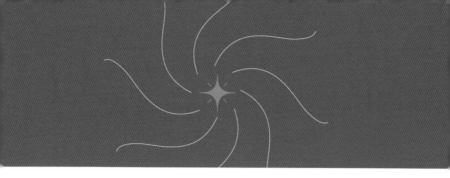

Consider your first goal.

Ask yourself: what's the value embedded into that goal? (This should be easy for you, as we found our values before we wrote any goals at all!)

For instance, the goal *I want to write a novel; I will write a novel; I am writing a novel...* leads us to the value of *creativity*.

Write that value in the centre circle. Now, in each of the 12 segments around the middle ring, I'd like you to detail 12 places where creativity (or whatever you chose) already flourishes in your life. Is your house beautifully decorated? Do you cook delicious meals? Do you take pride in your clothes, or match your bag to your shoes, or dress your kids in little outfits that make you smile? Do you love dressing up? Do you colour coordinate the apps on your phone? Do you always have a book on the go? Maybe you have a rich imaginative life. Maybe you can even feel your characters rising in your soul; maybe you write long captions to social media pictures; maybe you take beautiful pictures.

Maybe you go all out for Christmas or Hallowe'en. Maybe you doodle in your diary. Maybe you keep a diary. You've certainly been keeping this journal! Twelve places creativity is already thriving in your life; 12 places you might not have thought to be grateful for.

Now turn your attention to the outer circle. This is for the future, and we're going to write 12 ways creativity could be further welcomed into your day. Try to connect them, if you can, to the already-thriving spaces in the centre ring. Try, simply, to expand those things. It's always easier to build on a foundation than to start from nothing. If you already make beautiful meals, for instance, consider whether you might try a new recipe or a new cookbook. Could you write your own recipes down on a blog or in a notebook to hand down to your grandkids? Could you cook with a new ingredient? Could you write a cookbook?

If you take beautiful pictures, could you learn to edit those photographs? Could you sketch from those pictures? Could you write captions for those pictures?

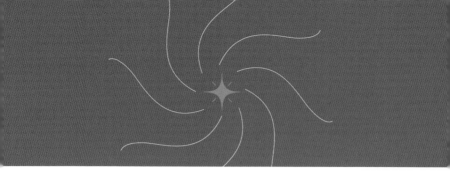

And if you already have the characters or an idea for a story in your mind, could you spend some time fleshing out those ideas? Could you make time for that? Could you write a hundred words every day? A sentence every day? Could that be the work you need to do for the universe to bring you your goal?

For each of your 12 creative hubs, you should write at least one expansion goal – at least one place where you know you could invite creativity to put down even deeper roots in your life.

Each day, we're going to remind ourselves of these 12 creative hubs; and each week, for the next 12 weeks, I'd like you to commit to just trying *one* of these expansions. Each week, I'd like you to focus on opening your home and heart to this core value that means so much to you. You must make time for your goals; and you must make space for your goals to align with your life...

INTENTIONS AND AFFIRMATIONS

INTENTION MEDITATION

So let's move, now, to an intention meditation. This will help us to commit to those actions. We will have to work to make these goals happen. *We* will have to try our best, too: it's not just the universe landing success in our lap. We must begin each day with a commitment to ourselves.

We write our Journal; we solidify our goals, and hopes. We commit to our vision of the future, and for that to work we need to commit to the work necessary to get us there. This is where an intention meditation comes in.

It has been said that the "best intentions can be carried out in a single second, and contemplated for hours". This means that you can take action right now to make it happen, but you

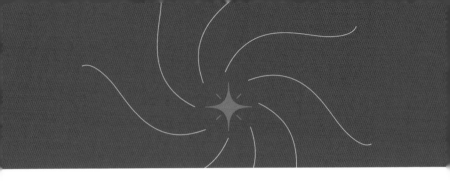

can also consider the longer-term impact of your choices and behaviour. An *intention* should be something that expands to fill the space available – and that can be compressed to fill the time available!

For example, if you long to be more creative – as above – you can take five minutes right now to make a quick sketch, write a few sentences in your Journal or figure out something beautiful to make for supper. But you can also sit down, meditation-style, with a candle flame and wonder: *How can I make more space for this in my life? What does it mean to live a life where creativity is the main focus? How can I commit to this goal?*

Let's begin each day with a simple intention, perhaps after we have written out our goal for the day, and checked in with the focus wheel. What actions will you take today towards your goal? What will you do today that will help your goal? What is today *for*?

This isn't forever. It's just for today. Don't panic.

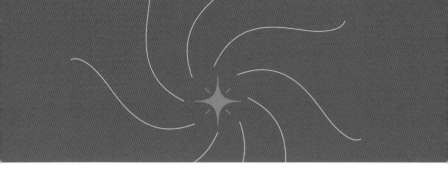

But ask yourself:

To what do you dedicate this day? To what, or whom, do you dedicate each breath of the day? To where does your energy flow - and from whence does it come?

Look at yourself in the mirror, and say aloud:

Today I commit myself to...

Like a priestess of some ancient religion, like a person with a purpose, you move forward in this world. You move toward your goal; and you have everything you need to achieve it.

AFFIRMATION MEDITATION

But how to make yourself believe this? It's all very well me saying it, but you have to know it to make this work. What you put out, you get back in: the energy you project will be the energy people meet you with. If you come in smiling, people will smile back. If you believe you're in charge, people will defer to you. If you believe you're worthy of kindness, people will be kind to you –and if they aren't, you will have the courage and strength to leave those situations. You must understand your own worth, and this is where the affirmation meditation comes in.

The final exercise in this book is designed to give you the courage to believe in everything you've written so far. It's incredibly simple.

Ask yourself: who are you, at your best? Take a page of your Journal, and jot down some words. Who is your best self? What goals is she meeting? What joys, and what successes, are hers? What qualities does she represent? What values are you embodying?

What did your inner child give you? What did your future self teach you? What does your present self know to be true?

Write them all down, as they come to you, as they came to you throughout this journey:

Funny
Beautiful
Lovable
Strong
Capable
Special
Playful

Independent
Creative
Curious
Kind
Loyal
Questioning
Generous

Smart
Beloved
Magical
Unique
Brave

Light a candle, maybe, or just meet your own gaze in the mirror. All those words above? No matter which ones you wrote down? You embody them all. You have all those things within you: we all do. I promise you it's true. You can manifest all these qualities in your life, and you will. *You have abundance; you have always had abundance. Everything you want is within you.*

Meet your own gaze, and say this:

Everything I want is within me.

Meet your own gaze, and say this:

I am enough.
You are enough, and you
are everything.

Pick your favourite of the words you wrote down, and say it aloud. Say it again, and keep saying it. Say brave, say curious, say beloved. Say it loud and clear, into your own gaze or the candle flame:

Brave, curious, beloved.

Find the word that speaks to you and your goals; and now affirm it to and for yourself.

I am brave.
I am curious.
I am beloved.

Say it again; say it with your name. Say:

I, Kitty Guilsborough, am brave.
I, Kitty Guilsborough, am curious.
I, Kitty Guilsborough, am beloved.

Oh, I know you feel silly. But don't you also feel strong? Don't you also feel, just a little bit, like the more you say it, the more it's coming true? I want you to say it until it comes true. I want you to say it every day until you believe in it; I want you to say it every day until your belief is the truth. I want you say it until you have spoken the truth into existence; and the world into being.

Everything you want is within you. You just have to believe it. When you believe it, the world will, too; and when the world believes it, it will give you everything you are owed: everything and more.

It will give you your dreams. And you will deserve them all.

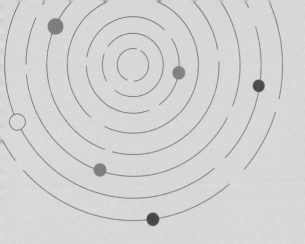

I create the life I deserve.

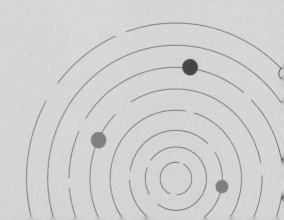

LIVING THE DREAM

So we have our goals; we have our plan; we have a strong sense of who we are, and what we want, and a map to where we are going. It's time, now, to live that journey.

In this final chapter, let's begin to live the dream together– no longer in our workbooks, but in our real, tangible selves. Let's feel the dream of our best selves in our physical bodies, and practical lives.

For whoever we are, and whatever our goals are, there are some things we all have in common. We need to eat; we need to sleep; we need to move. We need love, and to love. We need to feel part of a community. We need to belong in our bodies, and in the places we find ourselves.

And this quest, too, must form part of our goals – whatever those goals might be. Whether our goals are financial, romantic, career-based or creative, the best thing we can do to achieve them is to be the best version of ourselves. And to be the best version of ourselves doesn't need to be as daunting as it sounds: a journey of a thousand miles starts with a single step. And we can start those steps today. In fact, we *must* start those steps today.

Everything we've talked about over the course of this book – every dream, every soft hope and vague longing translated by now into a concrete goal – needs us to start from a place of self-love, self-belief, and self-care.

Self-care has sort of been hijacked by the millionaire hippie set to mean buying things like crystal rollers, and hundred-dollar candles that, when lit, smell almost as nice as a fresh load of clean laundry: a sense of self-indulgence, rather than self-care. And it's not that there's no room for self-indulgence. Part of good care is indulgence, the way you might sometimes buy a child a pastry on the way home from school rather than making them wait until they get home for a plain cheese sandwich. And yet, that's not all it is. Self-indulgence is an element of self-care, but it's so much more than that. Actually, it's so much more basic than that.

Think of that imaginary child and her pastry: she needs more than that, right? She needs boundaries, and a bedtime, and space to run around, and freedom to play. That imaginary child is your inner child,

the one we met back in Chapter 4, and she needs you. She needs you to love her: not just the way she thinks, but the body she lives in.

And maybe this is hard for you to hear. Maybe you recoil a little from the idea of loving yourself, and loving your body. And that's okay, too. We live in a world where it's hard to love your body, especially if you're a woman, and especially if your body doesn't conform to a narrow set of beauty standards. Every day, we're bombarded with ideas and images of how we should look, and what our bodies should be able to do. Every day, we're told that some bodies have worth; and other bodies don't.

Even something as fundamentally ordinary as wearing clothes, a basic human need, tells us that there's a right and a wrong way to have a body. Most high-street clothes are designed to fit one size and shape of person, and then simply scaled up or down through a simple ratio. Those clothes don't change shape; they don't change proportionally– so if you're bigger or smaller than the sample size, chances are they won't fit right on you. That is, of course, if your "size" is even available in the store. Lots of bodies just can't wear clothes from high street shops at all; the average-sized woman is at the

Part of good self-care in indulgence, but it's so much more than that. And actually it's so much more basic than that.

To live the dream we have to live it. We have to embody that future self we so long to be.

top end of the range many shops carry. Lots of bodies can't access these shops because they aren't wheelchair accessible, for instance; lots of bodies just can't afford to go in, or are afraid that they won't be welcome there. If you're not thin, if you're not white, if you're disabled, if you live in any way outside the gender norms– even if it's just wearing trainers where society hopes you'll wear high heels – you're fighting an uphill battle every day. And that's just one facet of life: one way in which it's hard to have a body. And if it's hard to have a body, it's even harder to love it.

So I get it: I get it, if you recoiled from this heading, and these paragraphs. I get that it might feel like, maybe, you came to manifesting because you're a person who lives in your mind, who spends a lot of time with her dreams of what the future might look like. Maybe you came here to try and get away from how hard it feels to have a body: to escape just this that I'm asking you to do right now.

But to live the dream, we have to live it. We have to embody that future self we so long to be, and we have to start now. We have to be in a physical state to accept the opportunities that present themselves: we have to be ready when they come. We have to physically prepare ourselves, as well as mentally.

So let's look at the big basic ones for the body itself: sleep and exercise. Sleep is when the body repairs itself; and exercise is when the body improves itself.

Diet, of course, is a huge factor too, fuelling those two as it does, but that's much more complicated – and controversial – to diagnose through the pages of a book. Eat enough; eat plants; take vitamins if you need to, and don't worry too much about it.

WHAT ABOUT
SLEEP?

We don't know how sleep works. A mad fact, but a true one: we don't know why sleep helps us, we just know that – by every conceivable metric – it does.

When we don't sleep, we die; when we don't sleep well, we don't function well either. Every new parent and late-shift worker knows the fug of being up all night; indeed, the UN treats sleep deprivation as an actual form of torture.

When we sleep, our bodies heal. In sleep, our bodies release hormones that mend our muscles, tissues and bones; in sleep the proteins in our bodies synthesise more efficiently; in sleep adenosine, a chemical that builds up in the brain through the day, is cleared away. We grow; we clean house; we refresh, and of course, we dream.

And so, to bring those dreams to reality, we must take the time to focus on sleep. We must take the time to rest, and begin again. We have a duty to ourselves, and our future selves, to take this seriously. Are you sleeping properly? Are you sleeping well? What could you do to improve your sleep?

The mnemonic STAR might help. Here are four things we can think about to improve the quality of rest: **Stimulants**, **Technology**, **Ambience** and **Routine**. Two easy things to avoid, and two easy things to aim for. Give your tomorrow self this gift.

STIMULANTS

There are two things we can do the day before to increase our chances of a good night's sleep: ditch the alcohol, and ditch the caffeine. One of these is obvious – we know that caffeine seems to wake us up – but did you know that caffeine works not by removing the adenosine from our brains, but simply by temporarily preventing us from feeling it? The adenosine still builds up – it's simply that we don't feel it. Until, of course, we do, and we're hit all at once by exhaustion that we can't do anything about because we're still too wired to sleep.

Ditch caffeine; and ditch the booze too. We sometimes think that alcohol might help "knock us out" – but passing out just doesn't do the same job, neurologically speaking. Plus, of course, you're giving your tomorrow-self not a gift, but a hangover. Getting rid of stimulants from your life is an easy win, and a great place to start.

TECHNOLOGY

Screens, like phones, TV and laptop screens, emit blue light. Blue light is typically produced in nature in the middle of the day; and so when our brains – little tiny animals that we really are – see that blue light, we think it's the middle of the day. We wake up. We can't sleep. There's a simple solution here: ditch the bedtime screens.

For two hours pre-sleep, try going old school and read a book instead of looking at your phone or watching TV. If you really can't manage this, it's also worth looking into sunset settings for your computer and phone screens. Or even investing in a pair of blue-light glasses to soften the glare.

AMBIENCE

One of the best things you can do for your sleep is to make your sleeping place just that: a place just for sleeping. No screens in the bedroom! Don't read in bed; don't watch telly in bed; and don't, ever, work in bed. If you're awake in the night, take yourself off to the sofa with a cup of herbal tea, and read there until you feel sleepy.

This is sleep hygiene: the idea that our minds strongly associate certain places with the things we do there. If we make our bedrooms places that feel safe, clean and cosy, we're likely to feel better about falling asleep there. And the more we do just simply fall asleep there, the easier it gets.

This is a true collaboration with your future self; every day that you only use your bedroom for quiet rest, the easier it will be to sleep tomorrow night.

ROUTINE

Which brings us to the last, and nicest tip for sleep: routine. Try investing in some bath oils, and some nice pyjamas. Maybe some nice bedsheets, too. Make your bedroom feel safe, and start signalling to your brain that it's time to start winding down. We're so vulnerable when we sleep that it makes sense that our little animal minds don't want to sleep unless we're sure it feels ok – and a routine is a great way to train your brain into understanding that.

Taking a bath with lavender oils at the same time each night; changing into sleep clothes; and going into the same sleep space? That teaches your brain that sleep is not only desirable, but possible.

ALL ABOUT
EXERCISE

Thirty minutes of heart-rate-raising movement a day can substantially reduce our risk of ill-health; but even ten minutes of simple movement makes a huge difference too. A sedentary lifestyle is a huge risk factor for things like heart disease; but it's also a real contributor to depression and a sedentary mindset. But you know all this, don't you? You don't need me to tell you of the benefits of exercise: I'm pretty sure you've heard about them all your life. You know that people need to exercise, you know that a body needs to move in order to feel good physically and mentally. You know you should, but maybe it's hard. Maybe it even feels impossible. So, one of the worst things I think this book could do is nag you about why you should exercise, and what it can do for you. If you're a person who loves the gym, you don't need to read this section, but if you're

a person– like me– who still has traumatic flashbacks to school PE lessons, let's think about how we can make this kind of thing feel good instead of stressful. The body needs less stress, and more joy.

How can we make exercise feel not like an enemy, but like a friend? How can we make healthy movement feel like something we want to do, not something we have to do? The mnemonic PREP might help: here are four things we can think about to make exercise feel more possible for us. So let's move: let's move with **Playfulness, Regularity, Ease, and Purpose.**

PLAYFULNESS

What if exercise was fun? That's the dream, right – that there's a world in which we can give ourselves permission to enjoy what happens in our bodies when we move. What if we took a more playful attitude to the whole thing? What if, like kids do, we tried all kinds of exercises – not just going for a jog, but boxing or ballet? What if we made ourselves feel good when we did them? What if we wore clothes that made us feel good when we did them? What if we didn't just throw on ratty leggings and an old shirt, but instead something that made us happy? What if we even brought a friend along with us? Someone to motivate us?

Let's try to remember what makes us happy – flick back through your journal – and see how we can incorporate that into our exercise. Maybe you love being outdoors and take up wild swimming; maybe you love being warm indoors and try a gentle at-home yoga video right there on the living room cabinet. Maybe you love bright colours and wild nights out – and could try a dance class. Maybe you love spending time with your kids, and could try a family cycle. How can you make this fun? How can you make this playful?

REGULARITY

Just like sleep – which, incidentally, is hugely helped by exercise – the more we exercise, the more we're going to exercise. Brains love habits, and if we can make exercise a habit we're more likely to do it. Incorporate exercise into your daily routine: set a time for it, and set a timer to go off on your phone. Early morning? Just before dinner? After you put the kids to bed? Set a time, and stick to it. Apocryphally, it takes something like sixty-six days to make a habit– and in the grand scheme of things, what's two months? Give it two months, and remember, take it a day at a time. Thank your yesterday self. Help out your future self.

EASE

Help your future self by making exercise easy. Don't put barriers in the way of your future health and happiness; and give your tomorrow self the gift of time: make things easy, make things natural, make things as convenient as possible.

Invest in enough sports bras and leggings that you can exercise even when you haven't done laundry. Buy an exercise bike and keep it in the living room. Join the gym that's closest to the office, rather than one that's a little out of the way; or lay out your yoga mat the night before; or incorporate exercise into your life in a way that feels natural.

PURPOSE

Give exercise a purpose, if you can. Find a way to make it meaningful to you or a way to make it part of something else: train for a half-marathon that is raising money for something that you care about; join an online yoga class where each day builds on the things you learnt the day before, so that you have a reason to turn up today; run to have coffee with a friend; cycle to work; walk the kids home from school instead of driving.

Give yourself a reason to do it, not a reason not to do it. What a joy to be able to help the planet and yourself in one, to be outside in the crisp autumn air or summer sunshine, or to beat the traffic.

Give yourself the gifts of joy, meaning, and purpose.

Affirm yourself as you move. Affirm your right to take up space; to move; to breathe; to live; to love. Affirm your joy. Affirm your capability and your strength. Affirm yourself. You are the person you dreamed of being. You are becoming the person you began this book longing to be. You are she; she is you. I am her; she is me. We can do this. I can do this.

I can; I am. I can; I am. I can; I am.

These are the twin pillars of manifesting, bringing the physical in line with the spiritual, the outer in line with the inner. We shape our own realities: we have the chance to move the world when we move our bodies, and when we open our minds. Open your mind to possibility, and your heart to love.

Think: *I can. I am.*

I am. I am. I am.

I can. I am.
I am. I am. I am.

✦